The Sweet Puzzle

KANISHKA SHARMA

notionpress.com

INDIA · SINGAPORE · MALAYSIA

ISBN
Paperback 979-8-89556-324-3
Hardcase 979-8-89556-832-3

Dedication

To all the souls,
Who have grown too rooted in the earth,
And forgot to remember,
How the air flows.

Contents

Grand
भव्य 8
Countless Stars 10
Would've Been, Could've Been 12
Flower 14
Enough for Both 16
Supposed to Hide 18
Maybe Not Mutual 20
With the Breeze 22
Just, Don't Know 24
I Wish, You 26
Make me Rich 28
Chose to be 30
In Lover's Resemblance 32
So, let it be 34

Stars
सितारे 36

Just In My Head 38

Everything Went 40

Sunrises and Shooting Stars 42

In Depth 44

Point of View 46

Never Just be Friends 48

My Name with Yours 50

Sweet Puzzle
मीठी उलझन 52

Eternal Verity 54

Homesick 56

Above All 58

Guilty 60

Sweet Puzzle 62

Shelter to my Killer 64

Think I've Fought It 66

Guilt Game 68

Slavery 70

I Wish 72

Known Unknown 74

May I? 76

Boon in Disguise 78

I Speak, I Talk, and I will Show 80

The Room and the Audience 82

But, But 84

Rain
बारिश **90**

Tender Cuts 92

Heart-achingly Insensitive 94

The Drizzling, The Rain, The Downpour 96

Lust, Never Love 98

Heal My Heart 102

Acknowledgements *105*

Grand

भव्य

Countless Stars

15 November 2023

2:57 am

"Loss of presence
Embracing the distance
Endless reserves of patience
Fear of expressing
Guilt of hiding
Do I deserve this? I wonder,

Countless stars in the sky
I lost sight of one I was gazing at
Never realised it was the last goodbye
Even if it was the warmest
I hesitated how was I holding all the butterflies
I was precise they all flew the right next moment,

Still staring with feelings
At only your roof
Passing by our spot
Although I know
I will not breathe the air
Where you took a breath, too.

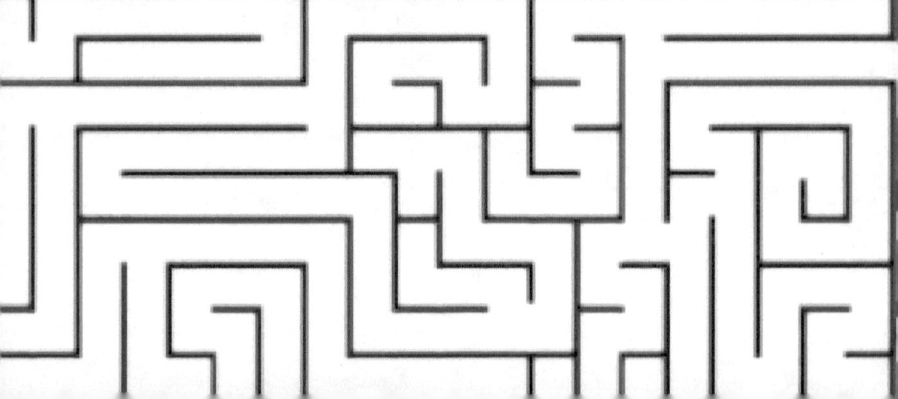

Would've Been, Could've Been

3 January 2024

10:23 pm

"Us is a feeling
I don't seem to feel
Limit is a thought
I don't seem to think
Your thoughts took all my nights
And days were gone dreaming
Something you were unaware about
Something we would've been

Fearless, I say I am
Wilful, you say you are
But still, I stay scared
Of waking up from this sweet dream
Where you eventually see
The agony and warmth behind these numb eyes
And where your only will is being with me
Maybe then you'll finally think about
My hopes and what we could've been."

Flower

16 January 2024

7:12 pm

"Plucked a new flower today
Wanting it to smell like
The one, I forgot,
Just to pluck.

I hold a basket of them
But the one I age to hold
Is always absent,
Some space in it
I'll always keep
As only that flower
Can make it complete.

I filled my pot
But forgot to water
Noticed too late
I lost the power
It disappeared
But once again I must see it
But for now, I can only make my pot rain
With tears and guilt."

Enough for Both

5 February 2024
12:01 am

"Hate me,
Hate me a thousand times
I would still want you
Only you, every time

Do it,
Take one million steps back
It's okay, I'll walk the whole world over
Just to get a single glance

Go for it,
Be with someone else
I would still think
Oh! You were just not in your consciousness

Tears in my eyes, I burst
They say you'll never love me back
But it's okay, I love you enough
For both of us."

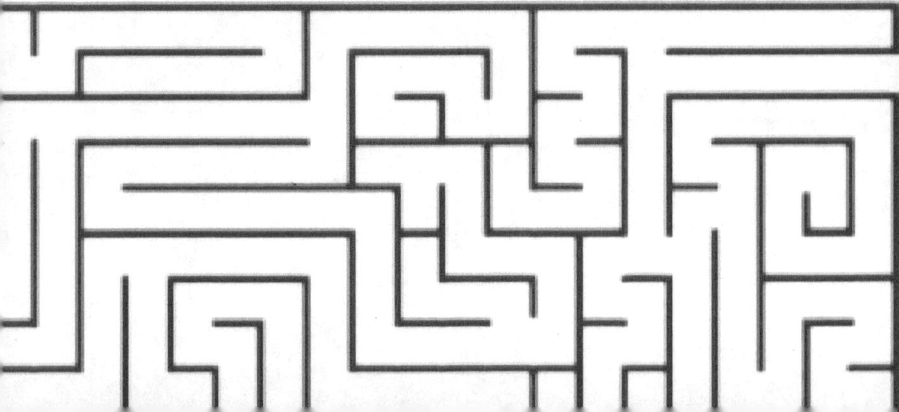

Supposed to Hide

27 February 2024

5:06 am

"Most beautiful form of love, they asked
One-sided, I replied
I tried expressing but
I forgot I was supposed to hide

Hide my passion for you,
Hide my belief
But the prospect of us
In my mind won't leave

How could I love anyone else?
Why would I?
I am unbothered by the distance
With the memories, I'm satisfied

Without illustration, I dream
Of you, non-stop
Your face is what I could envision
When I close my eyes, and hear a love song."

Maybe Not Mutual

5 March 2024

3:13 am

“Do you think about me too?
When the rain comes too strong
And the night goes too long
When you walk by our spot
And prove someone wrong

I wish every day
To wake up and see
It was all just a dream
And you are still here
Right here with me

But this can't be it

Maybe the feelings are not mutual

As you left me all lonely

With hundreds of people."

With the Breeze

25 March 2024

11:03 pm

“With the breeze, it will leave
The sense you created
The memories you gave
The dreams you nurtured
And hopes you made

I won't stay

But I will wait

Helplessly and almost hopelessly

Just in case."

Just, Don't Know

3 April 2024

6:37 pm

"I thought it was just a crush
Thought it would go away
I thought it would leave
Thought it wouldn't stay

But instead, it grew
Bigger than I expected
Deeper than I thought it could
Intenser that I thought it would

It’s not just a crush now
It’s in my breathing flow
It’s like you belong with me
But you just don’t know.”

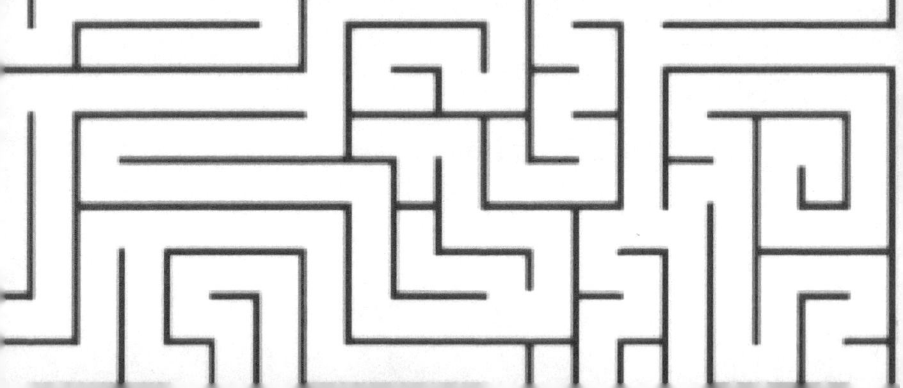

I Wish, You

1 April 2024

7:31 pm

“At every 11:11
On every new year
On all the shooting stars
With every aching tear
I wish for you
As if you are the only thing I would need
As if you are the only thing I don’t have
And except you, everyone knows it
When you walk away I always turn back
Ask the wind
The way I creep even in daylight
Ask the breeze
Where I have been these days
Proving that I am fine

Oh, ask my lord
How I forgot everything
I have known
And how tiredly I beg for you
to just come back home."

Make me Rich

3 June 2024

11:31pm

“Your grief is gold coins to me
Your agony akin to silver ones
Hand over them to me
And make me rich, my love

In your sadness, is my devotion
In your regrets, is my satisfaction
In your eyes, I see a rainy ocean
You see flaws, I see perfection."

Chose to be

10 July 2024

12:18 am

“My heart betrayed me
The day it chose to be yours
But on its way to you
It got lost

It was haunted
By your absence
But it has come too forward
Now to turn back

I told my heart
I am the only being it belongs to
But the hope it carries, my lord!
It's so stubborn just like you

It has become deaf and blind
Now, you're the shore and you're the sea
The day it chose to be yours
My heart betrayed me."

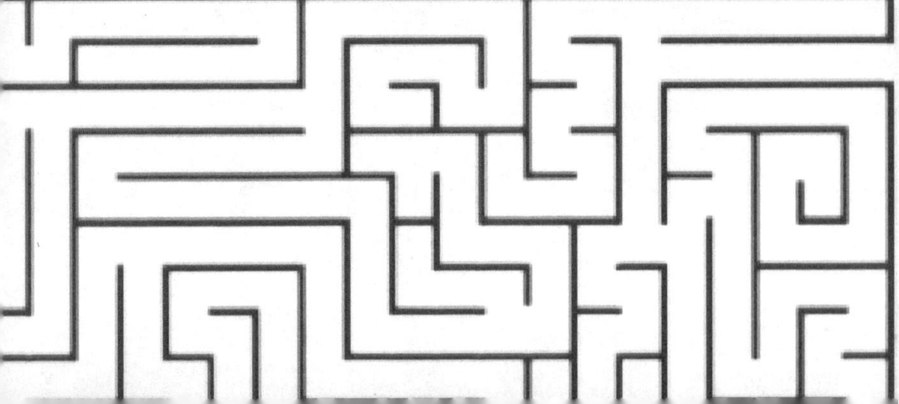

In Lover's Resemblance

4 August 2024

4:24 am

"The moon gazes upon you
And pines for its beloved
The moon whispers your name
In all its poems of love.

The rose yearns
To carry your scent
The rose must smell you
In its lover's resemblance.

You are life to dead
And peace to conflict
You are a wish come true
I didn't know I was making.

To eyes, you are destiny
To thirst, you are water
You are in every love story I read
You are an art and I'm a watcher."

So, let it be

11 August 2024

2:02 am

"Let your name
Be the reason for my life
Let your touch
Be the reason that I die.

The passion of my love
Shall increase
I'm not afraid anymore
So let it be."

Stars
सितारे

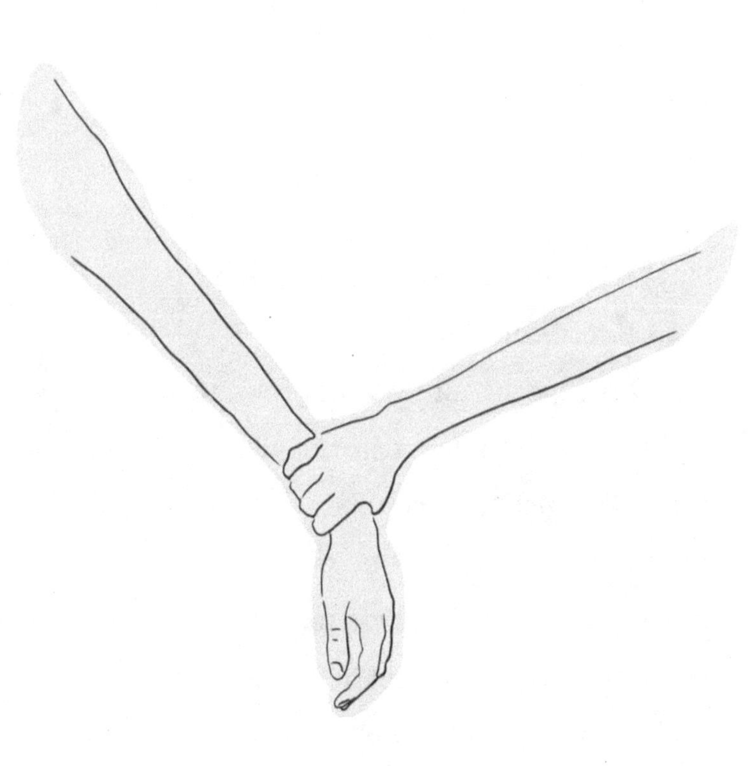

Just In My Head

14 July 2022

4:20 pm

“Maybe I’ve imagined way too much
It was never your fault
Now at this point, all I want is your affection
Maybe I was the sole creator of all those thoughts,
I guess you just can’t act like I want you to
Cause I’m not the only one who desires you
But the way you look at me makes me wonder
But in the end, it’s all just in my head
Cause I love you were the words you never said

Maybe I have expected way too much
That you'll drive me out of this town
And cut off all my pain
But now I guess I've finally found out
That it's all just in my head
Where you and I are dancing in the rain."

Everything Went

9 January 2024

5:19 pm

“Nothing exists now
Neither thoughts nor actions
My skin and feelings
are not mine I feel
Minutes seem like years
Hours seem like a century
Days Seem like an eternity
When does this time end?

I think I'll never be plucked

As there is nothing like "I" anymore

You are all of me

Not just the best

Along with you, I ponder

The pleasure, the bliss, the sense

Everything went."

Sunrises and Shooting Stars

26 January 2024

4:15 am

“I loved you at sunrises
You wished for me on shooting stars
Promised to love you forevermore
Hoping you’ll never go far,

Never said my words
But wanted them understood
By you and the whole world
Didn’t know you had some for me too,

Was too busy drowning in you
Now I'm paying the price
You may not see a shooting star now
But the sun will always rise."

In Depth

18 April 2024

2:37 am

“I was searching for you
While holding my breath
Didn’t know you were
In the air

I was seeking you
In the middle of the ocean
Didn’t know you were
Waiting at the shore

I was looking for you
In the skies and infinity
Unaware that you were
Right beside me

I was waiting for you
As usual in the evenings
Unaware that you were
Way far away, way in depths of me."

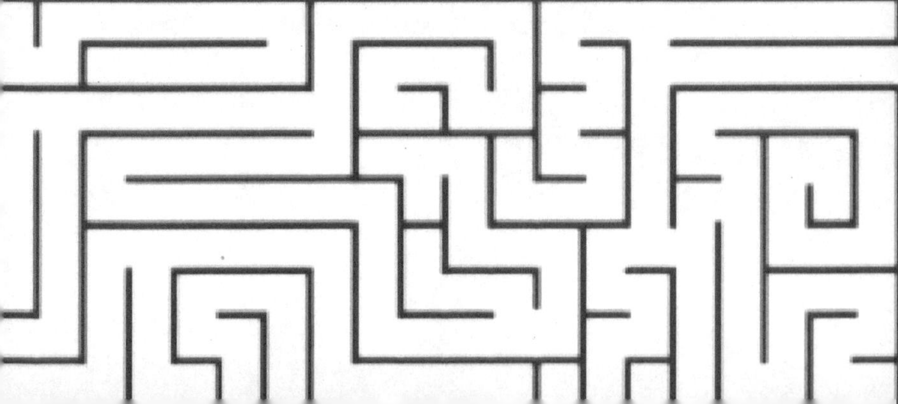

Point of View

29 May 2024

7:31 pm

“He’s so common
And I’ve never seen anyone like you,
He’s so childish
And I never have to care when I’m with you

He questions my every step
And you give me all the solutions,
He hates my taste in films
And I know I can watch them all with you

Love means nothing to him but entertainment

And if love were to be a human, it would be you,

He expects nothing less than perfection

And you say I'm a flower with a strong stem from your point of view."

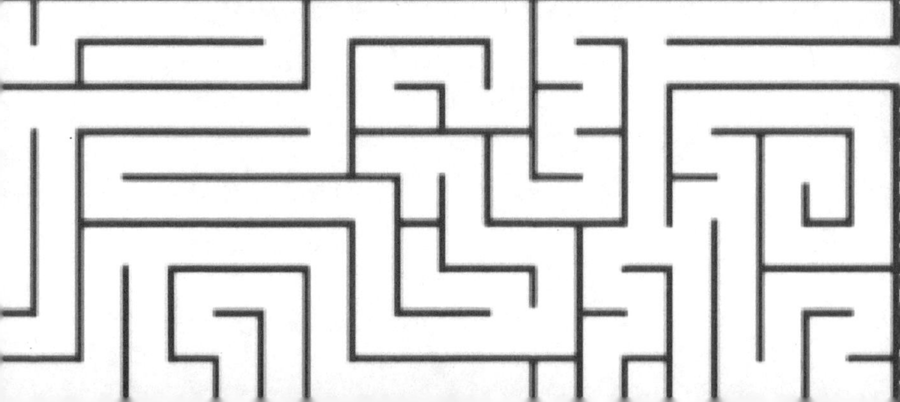

Never Just be Friends

30 July 2024

1:40 pm

"I'd rather say we have nothing,
Than to say we are just friends
Because I'm afraid it might be true
And then it would be the end.

Friends isn't just the right word
Because I search for my destiny in your eyes
We can never just be friends
Because I wish for you to see the things I wish to hide.

How can we merely be friends?

And why can't you ever witness?

That I attempt to save you, while

I'm tangled in strings of barren and hopelessness."

My Name with Yours

21 August 2024

1:51 am

"They said I'll meet you in the albums,
They said I'll see you in the skies.
They said I'll feel you in the nature
And hear you through the wind chimes.

But I meet you every night I sleep.
I see you on the reflecting surface.
I feel you when I touch my skin
And hear it with yours when someone calls my name.

They said I'd meet new people,
They said I'll just be fine.
They said it'll leave with seasons
And heal with time.

But I met myself
The day that I met you.
You hold all the colours
And chose to fill me with blue."

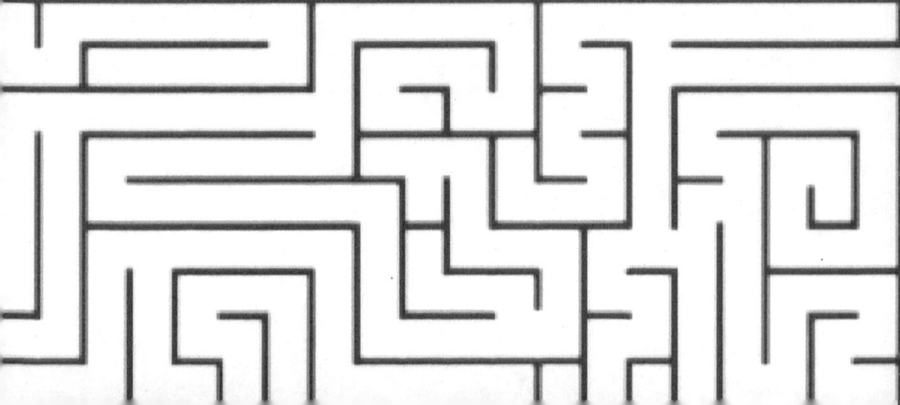

Sweet Puzzle
मीठी उलझन

Eternal Verity

14 January 2024

1:42 am

"Love is not
Something to have an end,
Love is like rain
It's over, you pretend

But deep in your soul
Where the eternal verity lies
A drop stays forevermore
But the chance to feel it's pleasure flies."

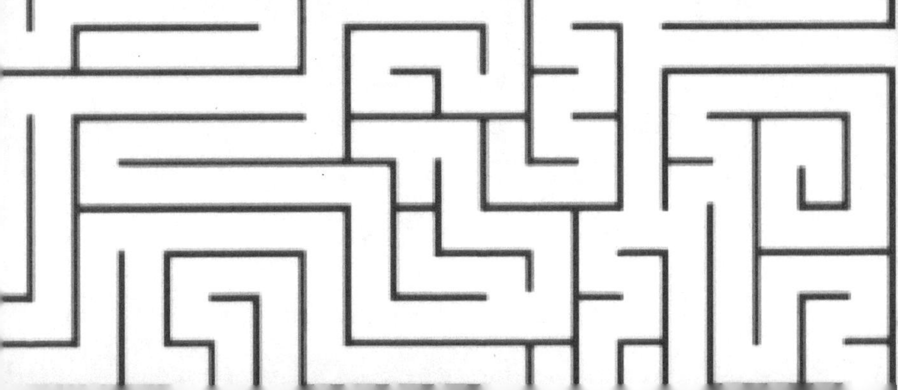

Homesick

15 August 2022

11:25 am

“Sometimes feelings can be so overwhelming
Leaving me homesick for a home I never felt
Exhausted from the endless thoughts swirling in my mind
Like a lost traveller searching for a way back

I don’t belong here
I don’t need to
I promise myself a place
Where I can feel free to

Express me
Without any debate
Till then I guess I'm just a traveller
On the wrong sea route

So, I guess they were
Right when they said
I'm just homesick of a home
I never felt."

Above All

21 March 2024

6:15 pm

"Everyone is waiting for my sun to rise
Unaware of the light my moon holds
They keep me safe in an aquarium
But I'm made for a sea, ocean
And everything bold

Everyone wants my train to run on their tracks
Unaware of the life my air holds
They keep me tangled in strings
But I'm born to fly
Above all."

Guilty

13 April 2024

9:19 pm

"Am I even made for "my" dreams?
I guess it's in my soul
Every person I ever meet
Their dream seems like a responsibility
Of mine to fulfill

Why do I feel so guilty?
For someone else's failure
Will it ever leave me?
Because I have dreams too that
I would die to achieve

Now and then
Tears come flowing
From my eyes
They ask me the reason
I'm ashamed to tell them why."

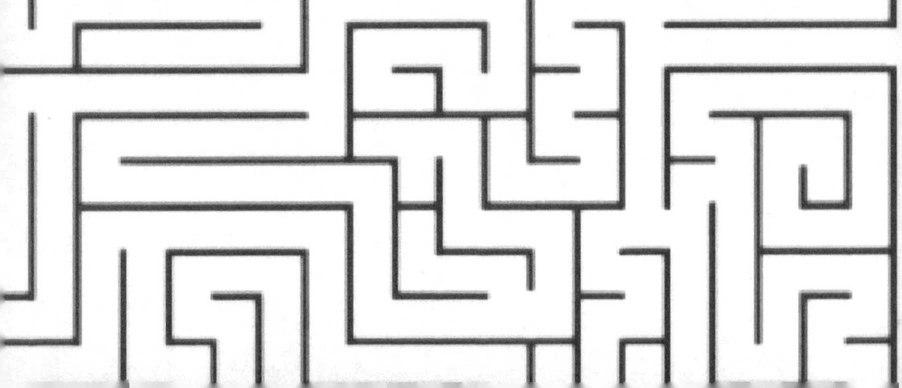

Sweet Puzzle

15 April 2024

5:50 pm

“The voices in my mind
The voices from inside
Are getting heavier and louder
And they aren’t even mine

I speak a puzzle
All in a hustle
But the voices make it sweet
Though they speak things I don’t mean
But if I did it I know I wouldn’t fumble

All of it had me
Break down to the floor
Tears fall in vain until
They are left no more

I will wear the chain
Leaving no complaint
The chain I refused to touch
When I was afraid of pain

I live in confusion
And the voices have a solution
It will certainly end me
But will also be my victory
And eventually, it'll finish my suffocation."

Shelter to my Killer

1 May 2024

11:34 pm

"What is mine?
Nothing I at last realized
When ultimately I die
Family and friends will cry

But after a while, they'll stop
And then I'll remain just as a thought
After all I would want them to forget me
And sooner or later set me completely free

What is mine?
Nothing I at last realized
The gardens I see
The air I breathe

The roads I go
The waters that flow
Will too, betray me one day
And that is for sure

What is mine?
Nothing I at last realized
The nature will offer its freshness
To those who hurt me or to someone else

I belong to nothing
And nothing belongs to me
As the tree, I love and rest under
Will one day give shelter to my killer."

Think I've Fought It

10 May 2024

5:10 am

"I think I've fought it
At least it doesn't bother me for now
This state I'm now in isn't very relaxing
But the fear is gone somehow

I think I've fought it
The battle nobody knew I was fighting
Never realized how much I wanted to conquer it
Day and night to myself I've been lying

I think I have fought it
But I'm nervous it'll make its way back to me
It's been so many years now it's intertwined
So, it hasn't really left, I think."

Guilt Game

22 May 2024

11:41 pm

"Letting go is the worst part
It gives you unbearable pain
Pain that tears your soul apart
And you can't even complain

You are left with no one to blame
But yourself and it kills to
This is the guilt game
Each minute in blue

It hurts you mentally and tortures you physically
Letting go gives you suffering unexplainable
The scars, the thoughts, the discoloration
Every sorrow invisible

You may leave the situation
But the clock hand will move
And time will make you face it again
Even in your dreams, it will haunt you."

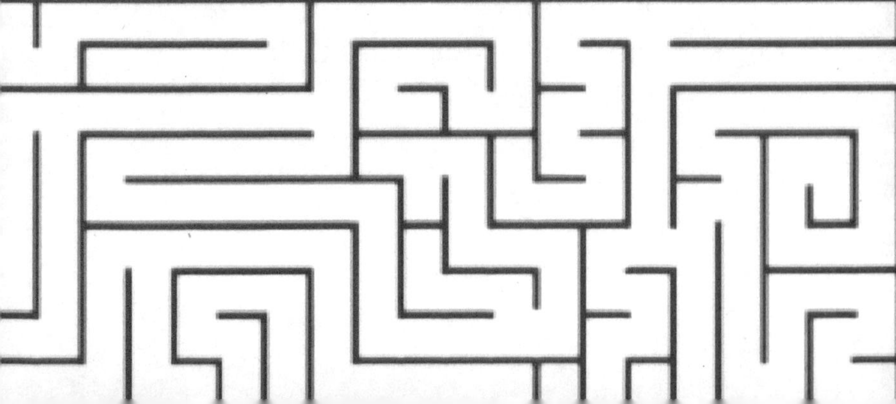

Slavery

31 May 2024

11:54 pm

"Slavery of mind
The minds of others as well as of mine
With time it makes its journey
The journey to the heart
Then flows with blood
and ignites every single part

It makes you feel disgusted
About the body you're in
A divine gift from God
And somehow you end up loathing it

We live in a society
And we MUST follow it
A rule made by our loved ones
And it thus leads to slavery

Different opinions are all wrong
Questions mean arguments
And if I don't play along with your song
I have broken instruments

As a child, I was born
But you shaped me with your opinions
My ideas and aims were torn
For your victory, I lost my definitions."

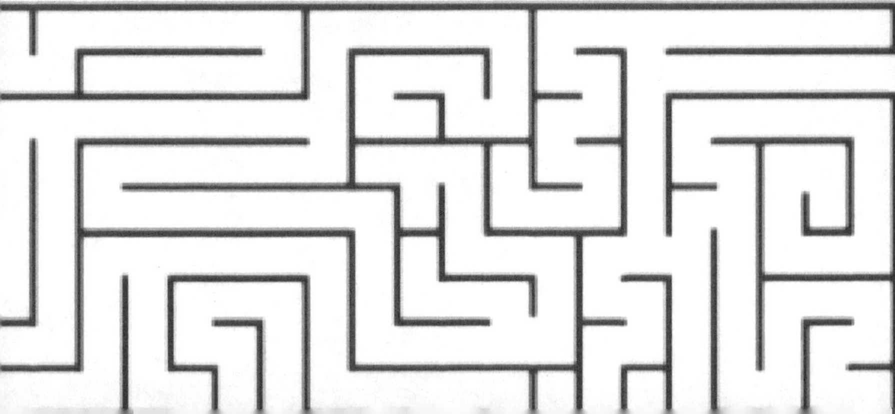

I Wish

9 June 2024

8:02 pm

"I wish sometimes
I wasn't the way I am
So, there wouldn't be many things
That I need to change

I wish sometimes
My only enemy wasn't me
So that stitching a heart they torn
Wouldn't be my responsibility."

Known Unknown

10 July 2024

2:25 am

"So, feelings mean nothing?
Until they are expressed
So, until it's shown
Love holds no significance?

So, talent does not matter?
Until it's properly displayed
So, care has no meaning?
Until it's explained

Then in this creation
What a clown I am
Making the audience laugh
Unaware of the reason

What a clown I am
To feel for the numb
And to love the blind
To optimistically perform before the untruthful audience all my life

To care so deeply
For someone, I don't own
To care so deeply
For the known unknown."

May I?

24 July 2024

1:20 am

"May I stay?
For the sake of being involved
Just to feel heard
Or would it be too unfortunate?

May I stay?

And not leave too soon

Shall I share some company now

Or would it be a bane for you?"

Boon in Disguise

2 August 2024

3:13 am

"In fear, I live
Fear of being behind,
Fear of making a wrong choice,
Fear of losing any time.

In fear, I stay
Maybe it's what keeps me alive,
Maybe it's what keeps me in the race,
Maybe it's a boon in disguise."

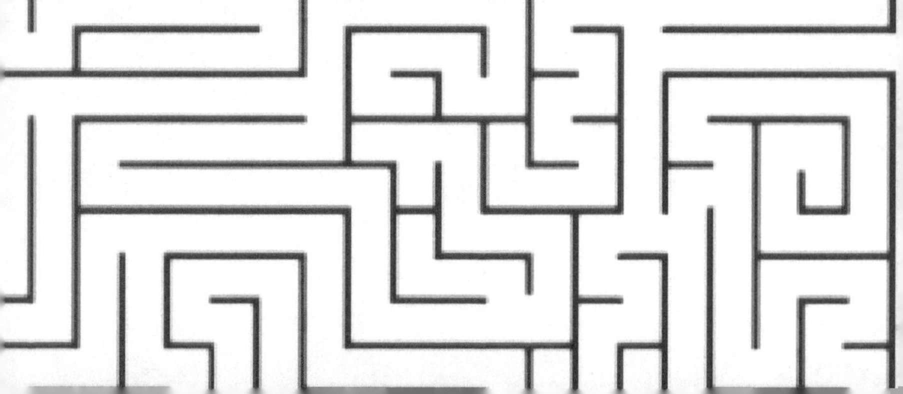

I Speak, I Talk, and I will Show

4 August 2024

2:32 am

"I speak my opinions and ideas
I speak my emotions and feelings
I believe in speaking for the humanity
But it all turned up against me.

I talk about my imagination
I talk about what the world Is capable of
I believe in talking for the quiet
But it all turned into "I talk a lot".

I am sorry for my words
Sorry that they overflow
But I just hope this one day
When I can not only talk but show."

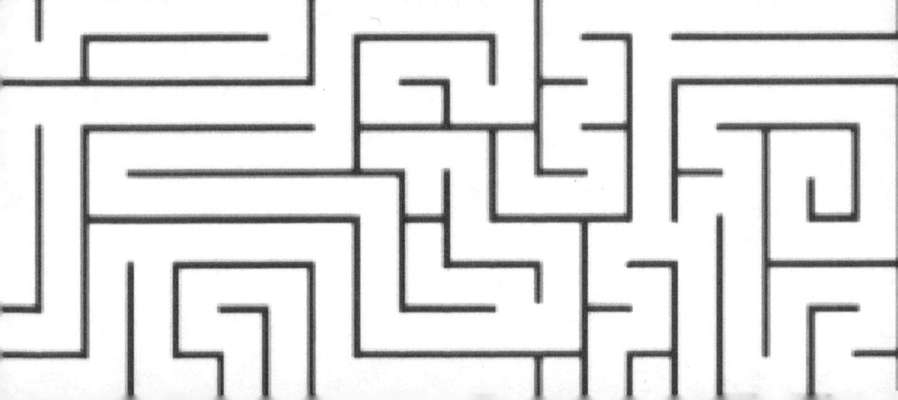

The Room and the Audience

10 August 2024

2:40 am

"Be happy and laugh
Keep everybody interested
The room gets full
And the audience decreases

Show sadness and
Let the tears flow
The room becomes spacious
And the audience increases

Yet we wonder

If humanity still exists

It might but surely have evolved

And I shall always persist."

But, But

16 May 2024

7:00 pm

“I know this isn’t the right way
In the present, my gaze should be.
Towards the future, I must see,
Counting each percent eagerly.

Making all your dreams a reality,
Bringing pride to all, faithfully.
This path I shall embrace
And I am ready to struggle steadfastly

But..

What if someone's comfort
Stayed in the past?
What if someone's love
Went with the wind too fast?

What if the past is the only place
I want to live in?
What if the memories are the only thoughts
I want to remain with?

Under the same collection of stars,
Just one more evening like those
My only wish, I swear,
Please make it last forevermore.

Hopes would come back
Flowers would bloom once again,
I will love evenings once more
Regrets will leave along with pain.

Just one more time
And I will never let it go,
Sitting together, smiling
Though not very close.

I'd still be missing you
While watching you right in front of me,
Because my heart's been aching for so long now
Oh! It's happening, it wouldn't believe.

But..

Oh, my lord, it felt so real
Dreaming my biggest dream,
Craving my biggest desire,
Which I know will never be fulfilled.

So, I will take your dream
And make it mine,
Work for the success
And for a life

Not sure if I want to live

But at least it will make someone happy

The grades and my package

All of it is too heavy

But I will count each percent

Worrying about the future that I MUST CARE ABOUT

Because I SHOULD LIVE IN THE PRESENT

As it's the only way you'll be proud."

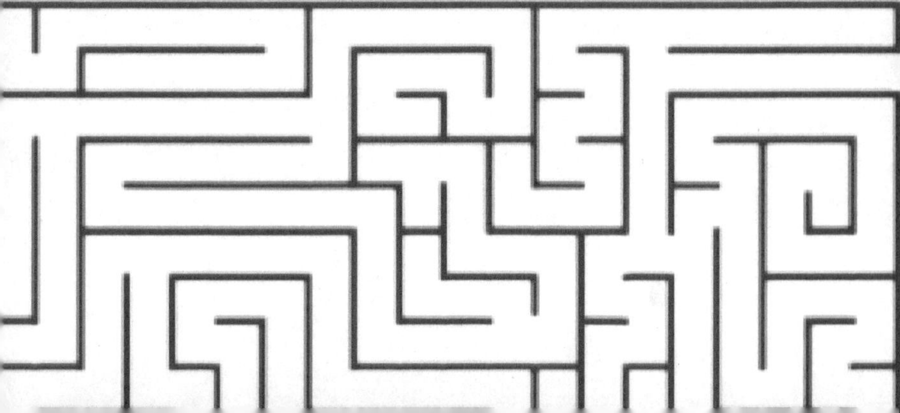

Rain
बारिश

Tender Cuts

20 April 2024

1:27 am

“When in the joyous state I am found
I look at them and chuckle a bit
Their gaze fixed upon me
As if my lack of sorrow
Is a grave error, they believe

I go about my business
Yet their watchful eyes remain
For reasons I hope are misunderstood
It turns into a debate, everything I observe
They inquire about my well-being
While prodding at my tender cuts."

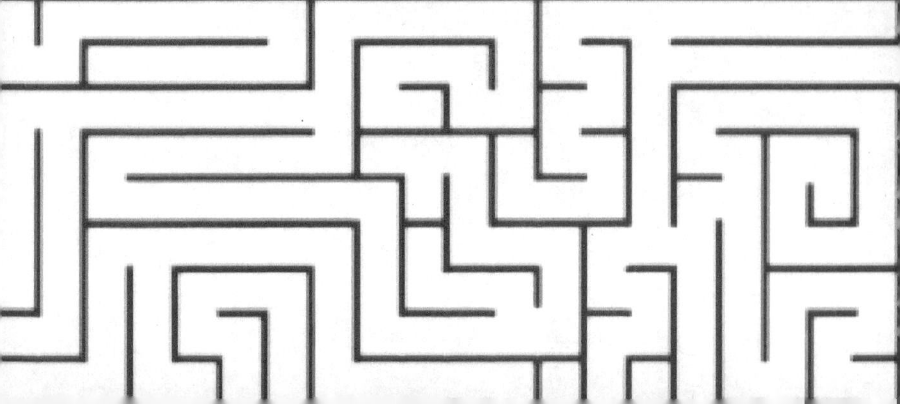

Heart-achingly Insensitive

26 April 2024

6:00 pm

"Don't explain your intentions to me
I can see through them clearly
I'm not naive or ignorant
Your actions are transparent to me

Don't help me comprehend it
Yes! I'm grateful for this living
Stop with all these excuses, please
You are making all the evenings depressing

Stop giving me points if
I make a point of everything
Okay I am an emotional fool
But you are heart-achingly insensitive."

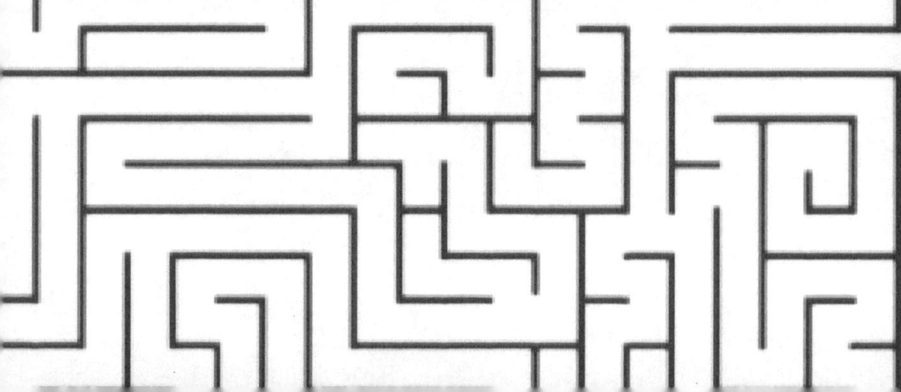

The Drizzling, The Rain, The Downpour

1 August 2024

12:33 am

"I ventured out into the rain's embrace,
Letting its drops seek me out with grace.
As moments passed, the downpour began,
Harming my possessions, yet I let it race.

I sought shelter and waited for a while,
Believing the downpour had ceased its guile.
Venturing out once more, I felt a gentle spritz,
But there was still a drizzling, maybe it's a style.

The drizzle ceased as night drew near,
Contemplating the rain, so pure and clear.
In the still of night, I quietly realized,
It was all just rain, in every guise."

Lust, Never Love

17 August 2024

11:57 pm

"So, it was always lust,
Never love?
So, it was just a craving,
Never a crush?
You stopped caring
Because I cared too much?
I wanted a connection,
But you wanted a touch.

Your eyes were filled with excitement;
I thought it was affection.
I thought you admired me,
But it was an obsession.
You didn't even try to hide it;
You showed it clearly in each expression.
I was aware of everything,
But I was running from a learned lesson.

Betrayed, I feel,

But you didn't cheat.

Are my thoughts right, or is there something wrong with me?

For once, call me beautiful and not perfect.

For once, let me sense my desired feel.

Because if we once lost this, it won't ever come back.

It's love, my dear, you cannot steal.

You don't know about my future plans,
And it's not even like you care.
You are uninterested in my past.
You don't know what I like to wear.
You despise my beliefs and
Never want to hear my prayer.
You say I'm better than all the other girls,
But I hate the way you compare."

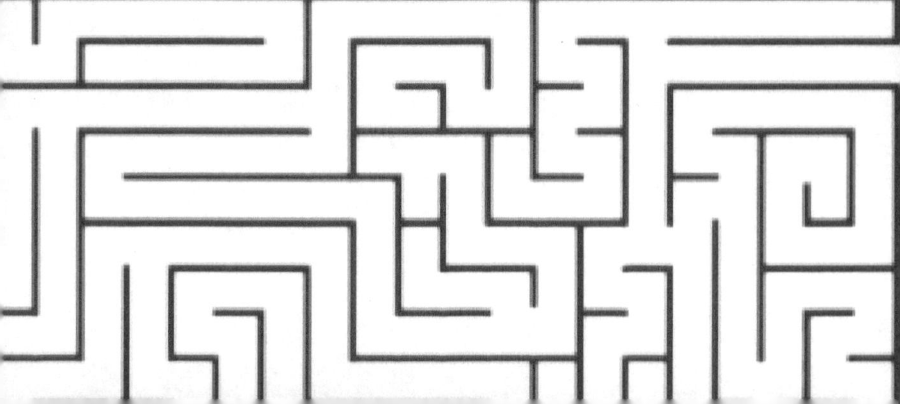

Heal My Heart

26 August 2024

1:25 pm

“Look me in my eyes
Let me win the battles because
I’m not the one I’m fighting for, so
Heal my heart by healing yours

I know it won't change

I stood still and endured

But I have a different wish now, so

Heal my heart by healing yours."

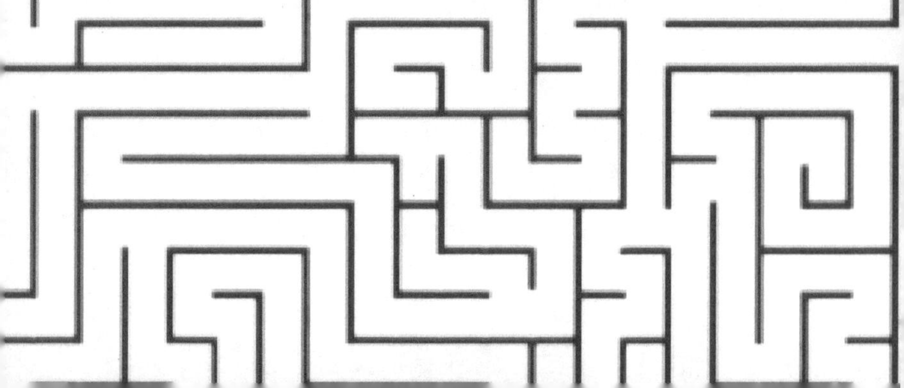

Acknowledgements

~ Readers

My greetings to every soul who took their time and gave "The Sweet Puzzle" a chance. I am heartily thankful for all the readers and grateful to share my writings with each one of you. Hopefully, I made a good first impression and if not, then I am sure I'll have plenty of opportunities in the future to make up for it. I shall stay for a while.

~ God

I thank my god for making me experience the truths of life and certain conditions which I most probably didn't want to experience but were essential. I thank my god for designing my brain in a very specific way which is my strength as well as my weakness. I thank my god for everything.

~ English teacher

I am immensely thankful for the presence of a truly remarkable and kind-hearted individual whose valuable contribution played a pivotal role in my quest for self-realization. The holiday homework assignment marked the beginning of all this. I'm so grateful for the shared times.

~ Physics teacher

Some statements have the incredible power to profoundly impact our lives, often without the speaker even realizing it. I wholeheartedly thank my physics teacher for being a ray of hope in times when I wasn't sure of anything. In some way or the other way, your words made me sure of what I am.

~ Family

~ Inspirations for writing.

THE SWEET PUZZLE

KANISHKA SHARMA

www.ingramcontent.com/pod-product-compliance
Lightning Source LLC
La Vergne TN
LVHW091114150826
845673LV00002B/815

* 9 7 9 8 8 9 5 5 6 3 2 4 3 *